MW01265454

Mary and Martha
AND OTHER BIBLE STORIES

BY REBECCA GLASER

ILLUSTRATED BY BILL FERENC AND EMMA TRITHART

SPARK
HOUSE
FAMILY

MINNEAPOLIS

Contents

The Lord's Prayer   3

Jesus and the Children   9

The Widow's Offering   13

Mary and Martha   19

Zacchaeus the Tax Collector   25

Text and illustrations copyright © 2015 sparkhouse. All rights reserved. Except for brief quotations in articles or reviews, no part of this book may be reproduced in any manner without prior written permission from the publisher. Visit www.augsburgfortress.org or write to Permissions, Augsburg Fortress, Box 1209, Minneapolis, MN 55440 or copyright@augsburgfortress.org.

Book design by Toolbox Studios, Dave Wheeler, Alisha Lofgren, Janelle Markgren, and Ivy Palmer Skrade
Colorization: Dave Wheeler

24 23 22 21 20 19 18 17 16 15   1 2 3 4 5 6 7 8 9 10

Library of Congress Cataloging-in-Publication Data

Glaser, Rebecca Stromstad, author.
   Mary and Martha and other Bible stories / by Rebecca Glaser; illustrated by Bill Ferenc and Emma Trithart.
      pages cm. — (Holy Moly Bible storybooks)
   Summary: "Illustrated retellings of several favorite Bible stories."— Provided by publisher.
   Audience: Ages 5-8
   Audience: K to grade 3
   ISBN 978-1-5064-0253-6 (alk. paper)
1. Jesus Christ—Biography—Juvenile literature. 2. Martha, Saint—Juvenile literature. 3. Mary, of Bethany, Saint—Juvenile literature. 4. Bible stories, English—Gospels—Juvenile literature. I. Ferenc, Bill, illustrator. II. Trithart, Emma, illustrator. III. Title.
   BT302.G484 2015
   232.9'01—dc23
               2015020852
Printed on acid-free paper

Printed in U.S.A.

V63474; 9781506402536; OCT2015

The Lord's Prayer

Jesus wanted to help people learn how to pray. "Talk with God," Jesus said. "God is listening! And you can listen for God too."

"Start by praying these words," Jesus said.

3

Our Father in heaven, hallowed be your name.

Hallowed means "holy." We honor God's name because God is holy.

Your kingdom come, your will be done, on earth as in heaven.

God's kingdom is where we experience God's love and follow God's ways. God's kingdom is in heaven, but it's here on earth too!

Give us this day our daily bread.
Ask God for what you need today.

Forgive us our sins, as we forgive those who sin against us. Admit the things you've done wrong. Ask for forgiveness, and forgive others.

Lead us not into temptation, but deliver us from evil. God is greater than hard times or bad things. God is always with us.

My Prayer

Write or draw a prayer of your own.

Jesus and the Children

One day a crowd gathered to listen to Jesus. Some parents brought their children to meet Jesus so he would bless them.

The kids played and laughed. They couldn't sit still. They wanted to see Jesus!

The children ran to Jesus and hugged him. Jesus smiled and laughed. He gathered all the children in his arms and blessed them.

The Widow's Offering

Jesus was with his disciples at the temple. They watched and listened as many people gave their temple offerings.

CRASH!
The richest people gave
huge sacks of coins!
They smiled proudly at
their offerings.

A widow came to the temple to give her offering. **Plink! Plink!** She gave two coins, the only coins she had. Quietly, she hurried back outside and went home.

The widow's coins were smaller than pennies. Color the coins.

Jesus asked the disciples, "Which offering was the greatest?"

The disciples remembered the huge sacks of coins. "The BIG offerings will help A LOT," the disciples replied.

"The rich people gave BIG offerings, but it was just a LITTLE of all they had," Jesus explained. "The widow gave ALL she had, just two coins. Her offering was the greatest of all."

Mary and Martha

Mary and Martha were excited. Jesus and his disciples were coming to visit! The sisters couldn't wait to welcome Jesus into their home.

Martha spent all day getting ready for the guests. She stirred and cooked the food; she washed and dried the dishes. "There's so much to do!" she exclaimed. "Why isn't Mary helping me?"

Finally, their guests arrived. Mary was so excited! She sat right at Jesus' feet, waiting to hear him teach.

Martha stomped into the room.

"I've done my share of the work today," Martha grumbled. "Let Mary help!"

Color Mary sitting at Jesus' feet.

23

Jesus turned to Martha and said, "Martha, you are worried about too many things. You only need to do one thing: learn about God! Mary has already chosen to listen, and I won't stop her."

Zacchaeus the Tax Collector

"He's coming! He's coming!" the crowds cheered. People lined the streets of Jericho to see Jesus.

On the tips of his toes, stretched high as he could, Zacchaeus tried to see over the crowd. But he was too short.

Zacchaeus was a tax collector. Sometimes he collected the right amount. Other times he took extra and kept it for himself. The people of Jericho didn't like Zacchaeus and wouldn't help him.

Zaccheus spotted a sycamore tree with branches reaching high above the crowd. He shimmied up the trunk and sat down on a big branch. But where was Jesus?

"Zacchaeus, hurry down from there! I'm going to your house today!" a voice called. Zacchaeus looked down. It was Jesus! Zacchaeus slid down from the tree.

Zacchaeus waved his arms. "Wait!" he shouted. "I will pay everyone back times four. I will give away half of what I have!"

Jesus smiled at Zacchaeus. "This is why I'm here," Jesus said. "I've come to seek out and save the lost. Zacchaeus was lost, but now he's found!"

More Activities

LOOK AND FIND

Find  in The Lord's Prayer on pages 3–8.

Jesus invited believers to call God "Father" as he does, probably using the Aramaic word *Abba*.

Find  in the Jesus and the Children story on pages 9–12.

Children were considered less important than adults, but Jesus did not agree.

Find the  in The Widow's Offering story on pages 13–18.

The widow put in two coins called *lepta*, which means "small" or "thin" in Greek.

Find this  in the Mary and Martha story on pages 19–24.

Welcoming others in your home was highly valued in the ancient world.

Look for this  in the Zacchaeus the Tax Collector story on pages 25–30.

The sycamore fig tree grows up to 65 feet tall. It has wide branches that are good for climbing.

ACTION PRAYER

Dear Jesus,

Thank you for teaching us how to pray. *(fold hands)*

We don't need to pray in a fancy way. *(wag finger)*

We can talk to you like a parent or a friend. *(point at each other)*

Help me remember you each day. *(point to head)*

Amen.

MATCHING GAME

Match the person from the Bible with the fact about them.

1. I notice people who are usually ignored and welcome them into my kingdom.

2. We often forget Jesus' instructions and make mistakes.

3. Jesus praised me for my devotion.

4. I was a high-ranking tax collector for Rome.

5. My names means "lady" or "mistress of the house."

6. People often treat us like we are not important.

7. My husband died, and I was very poor and didn't have many rights.

1. Jesus; 2. Disciples; 3. Mary; 4. Zacchaeus; 5. Martha; 6. Children; 7. The Poor Widow